WADHURST - THEN AND NOW

A STUDY IN PICTURES

STAN COSHAM & MICHAEL HARTE

AUGUST 2003

SECTION HEADINGS

ISBN   0-9545802-0-6

AN INTRODUCTION TO WADHURST

To those who know Wadhurst well, this view of the church of St Peter and St Paul and the nearby houses may seem familiar but not quite right - because it and Wadhurst have changed over the years. In this selection of material from the Stan Cosham collection, we have tried to illustrate some of those changes - going back as far in pictorial history as we can and ending with the events at the end of June 2003, when we celebrated the 750th anniversary of the granting of our market charter by King Henry III

The history of Wadhurst has been the subject of several books - some still in print and others only available from second hand book dealers or through the local library. The starting point for most has been the extensive collection of material assembled by William Courthope [1807 - 1866] Rouge Croix Pursuivant and Somerset Herald, whose manuscripts were bought by the College of Arms for the princely sum of £300. Most of the 110 volumes relate to genealogical material about Sussex families but three relate in detail to the church of St Peter & St Paul and to the history of Wadhurst and contemporaneous events

In putting together this selection we have not tried to be comprehensive or to produce a fresh history of our market town; rather we have aimed simply to entertain and hopefully to arouse an interest in the development of Wadhurst over the last 150 years

The captions to the material have therefore deliberately been kept short and anecdotal: those who want history should seek out some of the following:
The Story of Wadhurst by A A Wace [Courier Printing & Publishing Co Tunbridge Wells 1924] which includes the text of a lecture given by Mrs Rhys Davids in 1896
Within the Wood: Medieval Wadhurst by John Lowerson and the Wadhurst History Group [Centre for Continuing Education, University of Sussex 1983]
Wadhurst: Town of the High Weald by Alan Savidge and Oliver Mason [Meresborough Books 1988]
And there is a good selection of illustrations of Wadhurst, drawn from the Bocking Collection, in *The High Weald in Old Photographs and The High Weald - a Second Selection* both by Brian Harwood [Alan Sutton Publishing 1990 and 1993]

Charles Bocking was chief clerk to the auctioneers H J Austen & Sons and accumulated a mass of material about Wadhurst during his lifetime - photographs, ephemera and a series of notes under 600 subject headings. These he left to the Parish Council, which arranges occasional exhibitions of the material

Stan Cosham's collection has been built up over the last thirty years and is in serious danger of taking over his house; he continues to expand his holdings - by taking photographs of almost every local event and by getting material from all sorts and conditions of men and women, often as they are clearing out their attics or garden sheds. He also keeps an eye on the Wadhurst Recycling Centre!

The print that starts this book is a classic example of Stan's activity : it came into his possession in 2000 - in poor condition and needing restoration. The Charter celebrations provided an incentive to get this done and full size and reduced copies have been produced as commemorative souvenirs. The original drawing was done, probably around 1900, by Nellie Strutt, wife of Alfred Strutt FBA - a well known artist who lived at Rhosilli in Wadhurst at that time. It may well have been based on a very similar pencil drawing in the Courthope manuscripts, which seems to have been done from life sometime around 1850 - or there may be an earlier artwork somewhere still awaiting discovery!. From the left, the drawing shows part of the old Market Hall, then The Vine - now Twitten Cottage and Vine Cottage; next come Church House and Church Gatehouse - largely unchanged today, then the church with a different clock - the current one was installed in 1873; and, on the right, a house known as Town House or Clavers, which was pulled down in 1846 by Thomas Barton who then built the house now known as The Lodge

And the wide track between The Vine and Church House is now a footpath - The Twitten but then was in effect the High Street. Times do change - read on and discover many other changes that have left Wadhurst as it is today : still flourishing and better in some ways than in the past - but not in all

THEY PLOUGH THE FIELDS AND SCATTER

1. Ploughing the hop field in the early 1900s

In the Middle Ages, Wadhurst was renowned for its iron manufacture and agriculture was probably geared to the production of food for local consumption. By the nineteenth century, agriculture was the basis of the local economy. The 1801 Census shows the population of Wadhurst as 827 males and 850 females, living in 246 houses - as 308 families; 362 people were occupied 'chiefly in agriculture' and 136 'in trade, manufacture and handicrafts'. By 1831 Wadhurst had grown to 390 houses and 416 families - 1189 men and 1067 women; agriculture had 44 employers, 14 'occupiers - sole labour' and 324 labourers; manufacture employed none and retail / handicraft accounted for 119. Wadhurst also boasted 17 'capitalists, bankers, professional & other educated men'

Agricultural activity included the growing of crops, particularly hops, the raising of animals and the felling of timber. Now, alas, farming is no longer a major local activity and provides a living for very few. But hops are still being grown in the parish

2. Hooking the string to the top wire - 1940's

3. Thinning out unwanted hop bines - 1940's

4. Disease and pest control are always with us - sulphur spraying in the 1940's

5. Stripping the hops on the Courthope estate at Whiligh

6. Hop picking in Wadhurst

7. Stan's uncles - Dick and Tom Gunn - at the hop bin

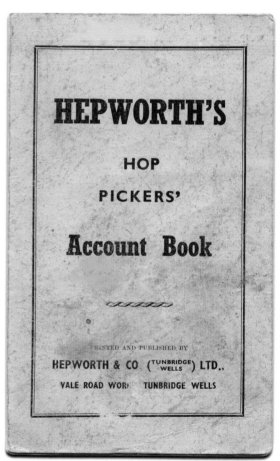

8. 1958 Hop Pickers' Account Book

Date.	Measurings. 1	2	3	4	5	Total.	Tally.	Cash Paid. £	s.	d.
Sept 15th	6	8	7			21	1/-			
„ 16	7	8	8	3		26				
„ 17	6	3	7	5		21				
„ 18	6	6	8	5		25				
„ 19	8	5	3	8		24				
„ 20	10	9				19				
„ 23	8	10	8	4		30				
„ 24	9	6				15				
„ 25	11	6	14	11		42				
„ 26	9	6	13	10		38				
„ 27	11	10				21				
						282				
								14	2	-

No. 60 Name Mrs Reed.

Binman

9. Mrs Reed earned £14/2/- for 11 days work in the hop fields in September 1958

10. George Davies at the hop press Little Bewl Water Farm in the 1930s

11. Hop picking in Wadhurst c. 1900
This time an all male group - note the range of clothing and of hats

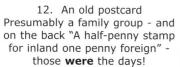
12. An old postcard
Presumably a family group - and
on the back "A half-penny stamp
for inland one penny foreign" -
those **were** the days!

13. Harvest time at Ladymeads Farm, Lower
Cousley Wood in the early 1930's -
they don't make them like this anymore!

14. Felling a Whiligh oak - as used for Westminster Hall in London
l to r: Fred Rumens - Sam Everden - Arthur Clarke - Percy Bassett - Bert
Kealey - George Kemp - Frank Stemp

15. Cutting the hay - today this would be called organic farming

16. Bringing in the hay at Whiligh

17. Loading the hay c 1908 at Whiligh
photo taken by Joan Courthope

18. And then making the hay
ricks for winter storage

19. Bagging the grain c 1970
Mrs Savage working on an old combine harvester
at Hook Farm Cousley Wood [submerged under
Bewl Water in 1976]

20. The Old Barn at Little Pell Farm
Covered storage was always a key requirement
for arable and animal farming - Wadhurst had
many old timbered barns, some dating back to
mediaeval times and others more recent. Today
many have been converted into homes or allowed
to fall into decay

21. Whilst others have burnt down
The Wadhurst Fire Brigade in action - Sub Offr John Walters with hose assisted by Bob Wilton
As The Courier recorded:

A farmer's son dashed through the flames in a blazing 15th century hay barn on Saturday to rescue 50 cattle, including several three week old calves, which he threw to safety over their pens.

The 20 ft flames, which swept through the barn at Greenman Farm, near Wadhurst, just missed the farmhouse, once a coaching inn.

24 dairy cows, which had just reached the farmer for milking at 4pm, were herded back across the Frant to Wadhurst Road to their field.

The owner, Mr F H Butt, was in London when the fire broke out, and it was the weekend off for the manager Mr R Hunt. However, he saw the fire from his home, and helped Mrs Butt, her son Graham, and his friend, Mr Christopher Gardiner, to rescue the animals. Firemen from Wadhurst and Tunbridge Wells attended, stayed all night, and left about midday Sunday, while 60 tons of hay were left to burn out, or were pulled into an adjacent pond. Several tons of fertiliser were also destroyed.

Mrs Butt said: "There was no sign of a fire when we brought the cattle in, then a few minutes later I smelt smoke. The whole place was ablaze in seconds."

The cause of the fire, which was still smouldering on Wednesday, is unknown. The Butts do not yet know the amount of the damage.

22. Bassetts Forge Durgates 1930
l to r: Tom Skinner - ? - Jack Bassett - ?
Farming supported many ancillary trades - the forge being a key business
in keeping the farm in operation. This one is no more - now converted and
extended into a small housing development

23. Rodney Bassett [l] and Andy Powell relaxing
in The Forge at Durgates in 1984 - Andy now runs
the Castle Forge

24. Fred Griffin - with haltered beast - at Walters Farm in the 1920's

25. The champion beast at the
Wadhurst Fat Stock Show
With Ted Finn [l] herdsman and
Michael Reid farmer - who was also
a light aeroplane enthusiast,
terrifying local cricketers with his
aerobatic displays

26. Hook Farm Cousley Wood in 1962

As farming moves steadily into decline in Wadhurst, some farm houses are converted into 'des res with all mod cons' - others are pulled down and new homes built in their place. But Hook Farm was drowned and the buildings demolished as the Bewl Reservoir was constructed. The 1976 water level is marked WL

GOD MOVES IN MYSTERIOUS WAYS

27. from an old postcard

The church of St Peter & St Paul has dominated Wadhurst for centuries - indeed until the later part of the nineteenth century the through road in Wadhurst went past the church rather than, as today, between the CHAT charity shop and the White Hart

The earliest part of the church is the Norman tower with major expansion and re-building in the 13th century [south aisle] and 14th century [north aisle and chancel] when the spire was added to the tower. Inside the church is noted for its iron tomb slabs, marking the fact that Wadhurst was a leading centre of the Wealden iron industry for at least two hundred years from the 16th century

Today the church is a centre not only for Christian worship as part of the Church of England but also through its participation in Churches Together in Wadhurst and Carillon Cottage, for support to the wider Christian community and to the population at large. Other denominations have their own places of worship - Roman Catholic at the Sacred Heart in Durgates, the Methodists in the Lower High Street [with other Nonconformist chapels now converted into homes - Strict and Particular Baptists at Shovers Green and Strict Baptists at the Rehoboth Chapel at Pell Green]; Crittles the Greengrocers was built as another Baptist Chapel - and only the Salvation Army is without either a home or, at present, a minister

28. The Parish Magazine for February 1959
The vicar of St Peter & St Paul was then the Rev
A N H Roscamp; the organist Kenneth Ascott
and the Hon Sec of the PCC Miss E C Potter of
Twitten Cottage

29. Advertising

As today in Focus, local advertisers were happy to
support the Parish Magazine - but none of these
businesses still exist

30. The nave and chancel of St Peter & St Paul
From a postcard produced by H Camburn Tunbridge Wells for R Perrem Durgates Stores

31. The choir entering the church 24 July 1985 for the induction of the Rev Michael Insley as vicar

32. The font - St Peter & St Paul
On the back of this ink drawing is written:
'Where Patric was baptized' - the son of the Vicar of Wadhurst Leslie Stevenson [1908 - 1920]

33. Inspection of the church spire March 1987
Steeple jacks Adam Geddes [top] and Peter Harknett
[lower] from Rogate Petersfield Hants

34. Inspecting the church clock 1993
Geoff Goldsmith [groundsman] and Roy
Albinson [civil engineer]

35. The Sacred Heart
Built in 1928 for the local Catholic community - before that they had
worshipped at The Mount

36. The Mount
Home of the Rosminian Order until the Rudolf Steiner Movement bought
the property in the 1980's as a school for children in need of special care

37. The Calvary
The Mount took its name from this Calvary, constructed by the
Rosminians as a counterpart to their Calvary at Domodossola

38. The Methodist Church Lower High Street
Built between 1874 and 1877 for the sum of £801

39. Methodist Fund Raising

Behind rail: [l to r] Mr R Roberts - Sharon Nutley - Ian Stead - Susan Elliot - LesleyAnne Swallow - Elizabeth
Partis - Richard Telford - Leslie Telford - Mr M Jones - Martin Stead
In front [from back l to r]: Linda Ovens - Janet Ovens - Barbara Clare
Denis Flower - Christine Flower - Nicolas Sherry
Kevin Griffen - Nigel Collison

40. The new Gospel Hall Turners Green 1971

41. By May 1987 the Hall was for sale
Now the building is used as offices

42. The Rehoboth Chapel in Pell Green
Built in 1824 and now converted into domestic accommodation. This
Strict Baptist congregation was founded before 1820, meeting in the
kitchen of Thomas Kemp, carpenter; outgrowing his house, the new
building was erected on part of his garden

43. Account Book
Extract from a set of account books
covering the building of the Rehoboth
Chapel - but starting in May 1819,
when the Baptist congregation used Mr
Kemp's kitchen and workshop.

Entries here include
Making a cricket bat 6d
5 days self 17/6
6¾ days boy 9/-
Carriage of 81½ feet of timber £2-2-0
A jug 12/0
4 Spittoons 5/0

44. Mrs Samuel Fairbrother's Funeral 1911
Samuel Fairbrother was a farmer at Walland and a founder of the
Wadhurst Salvation Army Corps
Leading the procession in a top hat is Mr C Ashby, Charlie Bocking's grandfather

45. The Wadhurst War Memorial
Unveiled on 8 May 1921 and
recording the names of those who
laid down their lives in two World
Wars - 114 in 1914 - 1918 and 33
in 1939 - 1945
"Their names shall live forever"

Unveiling of Wadhurst War Memorial.

46. Wadhurst High Street looking east - before the 1930's
Showing the Baptist Chapel - later 'La Collina' and now Crittles - on the left

47. Cousley Wood National School c.1935
The school became the local church - here the Sunday School is on
parade. Now the building is a private residence

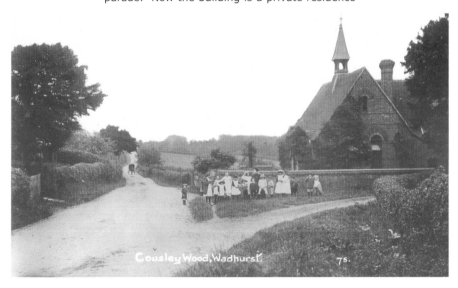

48. The Mission Church Faircrouch Lane
Originally The Iron Church in Woods Green - moved to Faircrouch Lane in
1898 and demolished in 1956: the site - almost opposite the Waste
Recycling Site - is now totally overgrown

49. Chapel in Shovers Green - now converted into a house

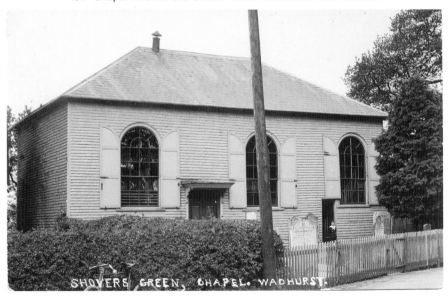

THE STREET SCENE

50. July 1990 - in the evening sun: taken by Stan Cosham from a hot air balloon
The street pattern in Wadhurst has hardly changed over the years - the High Street used to run past the church and Sheepwash Lane was widened to become Washwell Lane when Courthope Avenue and the adjacent roads were laid out for housing but otherwise little change apart from steady growth

51. The High Street looking west early 1900s
Notice the steps down to the shops on the left, a house in front of James
Rogers & Meridian Art, the old White Hart Inn where Ashton Burkinshaw
now operates

52. In 1905
The Queen's Head, displaying its splendid sign - and no traffic problem

Wadhurst, High Street.

53. Around 1906 - shaving available where Jean Marie now operate and the Queen's Head stables functions but note the internal combustion engine

54. Until some time around 1840 this gap was blocked by gardens - here Tea & Luncheon Rooms [now One Stop] at the top of Sheepwash Lane and CHAT was then a family house : the road was still a safe place for pedestrians

55. By now the pavements are getting better and the vehicles larger; the
International Stores has moved from across the road and Featherstones
runs a delivery service [now Wadhurst Flowers - who also deliver]

56. Looking west today from Wadhurst Ironmongers and 57. from The White Hart
Traffic is the major problem facing the High Street - parking is difficult and, when school comes out, gridlock
is not far away

58. The High Street looking east - 1907
In the previous century the main road went to the left down Church Street

59. 1918 Ashby - Furnisher, Draper and Grocer: now Lloyds Bank. On
the right, the Post Office [Castertons - who published this postcard: the
tradition continues today with Tony Tregaskes; the shop is now Jackie Martel]
and the butchers - now W J Crouch

60. In 1910 - suffering from winter snows. The trees on the right are
now the forecourt of the Wadhurst Institute

61. By 1928, Ashbys is now the bank and a garage has opened where
later Baldwins [electrical and radio] and now Magpie do business

62. In 1935 the horse and the internal combustion engine still co-existed; Gadd's Garage [now replaced by Wood-B-Pine]

63. The Walk - with no pavement and the old wheelwright's - weatherboarded on the left. The limes are well trimmed

The Walk — Wadhurst

64. The backs of some of the oldest houses in Wadhurst - from the churchyard

65. Sheepwash Lane - a narrow track leading up to the High Street : now Washwell Lane - the houses at the top were demolished and the lane widened in 1960 to provide access to Courthope Avenue

SHEEPWASH LANE, WADHURST.

66. The High Street - no pavement on the left and a different roof line and fenestration to what is now Lloyds Bank. And The Institute has a garden - where now we park cars for shopping and for functions in the Commemoration Hall

WADHURST: HIGH ST., & INSTITUTE.

67. Wellington Place 1905 - looking south
T J Barnes Draper & Grocer on the right [now Culverden the Vets]

68. Sparrows Green 1905
Newingtons [now Costcutters] on left and the old Red Lion Inn - selling
Duttons beers - on the right

69. Sparrow Green - a little earlier with building works ahead

70. Sparrows Green again - with H. Deeprose Fishmonger [now Wadhurst Rod and Line] then A E & M Streeter Tea & Coffee [now a private house] - milk delivery outside Health Bakery [now rebuilt]

71. Osmers Hill c 1910

72. Turners Green - even the children in hats & caps
perhaps on the way to a National Hospital Sunday procession

73. Durgates - looking west: 1912
Bassetts Forge on left - and notice the telegraph wires : no broadband
capability here

74. Durgates - when it was safe to walk in the road : on the right is now the
Castle Park housing development

75. The Balaclava Inn - Style & Winch beers on offer
still a pub - The Dobbin Inn

76. Durgates Industrial Estate
Light industry and service businesses have largely replaced agriculture as
the main employers : small industrial and business estates have sprung up
since the last war - either purpose built or in converted agricultural buildings

77. Bewl Water - marking the north east boundary of Wadhurst Parish
Photo taken by Stan Cosham from a hot air balloon July 1990

MUSIC HATH THE POWER TO CHARM

78.   Wadhurst Church Choir 1962

Back: Peter Boorman - David Chapman - Michael O'Shea - Mr Ascott [organist] - ? - Mr Barham
4th row: Miss Bryan - Miss Baldock - Margaret Noakes - Rev Nicholas Roscamp - ? - ? - ?
3rd row: Philip Littlejohn - Peter Wilsher - Peter Swift - Mark Littlejohn - ? - Richard Creasey - Richard Holland
2nd row: Stephen Sewell - Philip Easton - Brian Gill - Robert Madge - Stephen Baldock - John Barden -
Robert Holland - Richard Griffin
1st row: Jeremy Ascott - ? - ? - ? - Ian Lilly - ? - ? - Renfrey Ascott - ?

Music has played a part in Wadhurst life - in all sorts of ways, drawing in players of all
levels of skill and of all ages. Today the Brass Band and the Drum & Fife Band enliven
local functions and parades, music in Church - and the bells - brighten the round of
services. Choirs raise their voices to the roof but, alas, the hand bell ringers are having to
close as the younger generation cannot be persuaded of the delights that form of gentle
music can provide

79. The Wadhurst Town Band in 1928

80. And again a little later
Front l-r: -?- Stanley Manktelow
Seated l-r: Milroy -?- Charlie Manktelow -?- Jack Dyer -?- -?-

81. Another one of ours. But who and when?
Photo taken by Wheeler Fisk-Moore of Tunbridge Wells

82. The Salvation Army Brass Band Wadhurst in April 1910
from an old postcard

83. The 'Wets and Whistles'
Wadhurst Drum & Fife Band in
1984 playing in the sun at the
Primary School Fete
Bandmaster C Mitchell

84. The Wadhurst Brass Band
in 1986
playing in Tunbridge Wells at the
Pantiles Bandstand - Algy Hoare
in charge
The band flourishes, with half a
dozen performances or more
each year in Wadhurst and
across Kent and Sussex

85. Ladies' Choir concert - organised by Mrs Stevenson
Her husband Leslie was Vicar of Wadhurst from 1908 - 1920
The Drill Hall was where Kingsley Court now stands

86. Wadhurst Youth Band at Uplands 1978
- under the baton of Algy Hoare

87. Stan Cosham, Monica Jones
and the Wadhurst Trefoil belles -
handbell ringing to support the
Photo Exhibition in 1988

88. Salvation Army Band at Uplands - July 1985
Sadly the Salvation Army no longer has a presence
in Wadhurst

89. The choir of St Peter & St Paul in 1966
- at the back the vicar: Rev Donald Plumley

90. The Wadhurst Drum & Fife Band
On parade : Remembrance Sunday 1991

91.   St Peter & St Paul Bellringers 1984
Still ringing the changes today - a church without its bells would be sad

92. The 'down' platform to Hastings in 1908 - ready for a family outing to the sea!

It would be nice to think that traveling was better and easier today than in times gone by. In the days of the horse and cart or carriage Sussex roads were notorious for their appalling condition - not much change today. The coming of the railway brought competition and improvement to all forms of transport but the twentieth and twenty-first centuries have seen steady deterioration : traffic jams and delayed and cancelled trains are all far too familiar for comfort

In 1826 William Courthope recorded details of his journey from Rotherhythe to Wadhurst; he walked from Tunbridge Wells: "After proceeding about 2 miles....I found I had to strike out of the good road into a bye way and who can describe the horrors of the dirt....in the first place there was no footpath, in the next place there were four tremendous hills to go up, so steep that a cart with two horses that was going up over them at the same time as myself was obliged to halt about every 3 minutes"

93. Wadhurst Station - the 'down' line 1912
Notice the changes over time - in dress and in the layout of the railway
lines. Sidings and shunting lines have changed over the years - as have
the surrounding buildings

94. The Hastings train approaching
Fred Styles - porter - holding the step ladder - note the pedestrian crossing
control and the waiting foot passenger

95. The 'down' line in 1958
The building at the end of the platform has now gone - as has the signal
box and the connection from the siding to the 'up' main line

96. Again - in 1985
with Mr C Hook the station master

97. Did it really
cost £2.36??

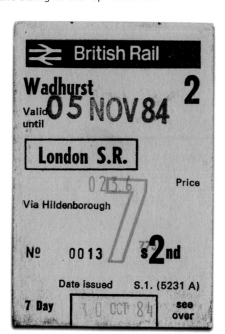

98. The morning rush hour - or is it an outing - c 1907?
Then - almost all men and almost all wearing caps

99. Station parking today
And this is the start of the holiday season!

100. The pedestrian crossing east of the station
The cottages were pulled down in the 1970s - today they would be
converted into commuter homes at £200 000 a piece!

101. The line past the Miners Arms
No longer a pub!

102. Station Approach
No parking - on the way to the seaside? The buildings at the west end
have now gone to make way for more cars

103. Station Approach looking east
The Railway Hotel was replaced by The Rock Robin - and the future of that
is in doubt. The coal yard was still in use - and the building at the end of
the approach has been demolished to make way for more parking

104. Station Approach
The station may not have changed but the surroundings have - see the
track from the main line to the coal siding, the goods track and the pile
of 'luggage' in the forecourt!

105. Again - notice the combination of rail and horse drawn transport
Safety regulations have clearly changed since this photo was taken!

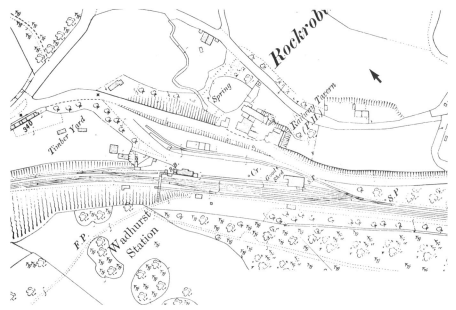

106. Track layout in 1909
The footbridge now shown replaced two turntables and a crossover line,
used to help load carts etc on to wagons and then move them from one
main track to the other. The coal siding and maintenance track and shed
are also shown to the north east of the main lines

107. The Hastings line
In happier days when you could
take trunks and wicker hampers
on the train - with porters to help

108. Platelayer's trolley
Useful when the train breaks down!

109. Inside the Wadhurst signal box
The white painted levers used to control the goods
and coal yards - the box was finally closed in 1986
and dismantled in March 1987 for re-erection in
Northiam on the Kent & East Sussex Railway

110. Sparrows Green c 1900
A more leisurely form of transport
- compare this to 'school out' at
the Church of England Primary
School today

111. A Victorian pony drawn hearse - with 'Peanuts'

112. Mending a puncture - or just pumping up the tyre?

113. Wheel collapse in Durgates 1935
E J Austen's cart with Benjamin Tompsett holding the horses

114. The entrance to The Fountain Inn Tidebrook
No drink driving laws in those days

P.J.LAVENDER. PHOTOGRAPHER. WADHURST.

115. Mr E Blackman
The roads may have been poor but they were
regularly repaired. This postcard, taken by P J
Lavender of Wadhurst, has appeared in print
before - but it is worth repeating
The Town Plan, prepared by William Courthope,
shows that Edward Blackman - labourer - lived on
the north west side of The Marlpit around the
middle of the nineteenth century

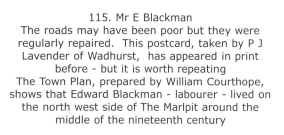

116. Road repairs - c.1905
And here is Edward Blackman at work - steam roller and all

117. Ben Greig's Garage
Sparrows Green 1954
The business has clearly
flourished - this building has been
pulled down with a complete
rebuild behind the forecourt. But the
telephone number has hardly changed
- from Wadhurst 157 to 783 157

118. Eaton Bros 1986
Best Beech
With Philip Eaton showing off a
new Panda. The business has
now closed and the site has
been re-developed for housing

BUYING AND SELLING

Buying and selling of goods and services are essential activities in any thriving community - they are also activities subject to continuous change. Few - if any - businesses that existed in Wadhurst a hundred years ago survive today : the shops change hands or are converted to other uses; houses become shops and return to domestic use

The High Street has been the centre of trade for generations but traders have operated right across the parish. The market itself may have disappeared and over the years changed its location - from around St James' Square, where the mediaeval Market Hall once stood to the auction hall behind Jackie Martel and the Pharmacy; that market closed in 1982. And the hurricane of 1987 wrecked the building : now we have a car park extension in its place

Wadhurst is well served by its shops and traders : there is little that might be needed for daily living that cannot be found in the High Street, in Durgates or Sparrows Green, or in the surrounding area - long may that happy state last

Please bring this Catalogue with you.

FRIDAY, SEPT. 27th, 1929.

Buttons Farm, Wadhurst.

About 3½ miles from Wadhurst Station and about 2 miles from the Ticehurst Bus Route.

CATALOGUE

OF

32 Shorthorn, Friesian & Cross-bred **DAIRY COWS**

6 Weanyer Heifers,   3-yr. old Shorthorn Bull,

MIDDLEWHITE SOW,

4 HORSES,   FILLY FOAL.

FARM IMPLEMENTS,

together with a quantity of

HOUSEHOLD FURNITURE,

which Messrs.

E. WATSON & SONS

have received instructions to Sell by Public Auction, as above, for Mr. A. E. Bussey, who is quitting.

SALE TO COMMENCE AT 1 P.M.

Auction and Estate Offices:

WADHURST & HEATHFIELD.

Phone No. 6.   Phone No. 11.

Cooper, Printer, Ticehurst.

119. Mixed sales were clearly commonplace - here Mr Bussey is quitting farming at Buttons Farm

120. And here Mr Langmore 'is leaving the neighbourhood'

WEDNESDAY, SEPTEMBER 19, 1888.

DURGATES LODGE, WADHURST.

CATALOGUE OF

A VERY EXCELLENT DUN COB

Quiet to ride and drive and suitable for a Lady,

A CAPITAL

VIS-A-VIS COB PHAETON,

A Plated Chaise Harness,

A GENT'S RIDING SADDLE AND BRIDLE,

3 CUCUMBER FRAMES & LIGHTS,

ABOUT 30 HEAD OF POULTRY,

QUANTITY OF CONSERVATORY PLANTS,

AND A FEW PIECES OF

HOUSEHOLD FURNITURE

And Miscellaneous Effects,

Which will be Sold by Auction without reserve, by Messrs.

H. J. AUSTEN & SONS

ON THE PREMISES AS ABOVE,

On Wednesday, September 19th, 1888,

COMMENCING AT ONE O'CLOCK, P.M.,

By direction of H. B. Langmore, Esq., who is leaving the neighbourhood.

Catalogues may be obtained of Messrs. Austen & Sons, Auctioneers and Valuers, Wadhurst.

Balcombe, Printer, Ticehurst.

Wadhurst Markets

CONDUCTED BY MESSRS.

E. WATSON & SONS, F.A.I.

IN THE SALE YARD AND MARKET HALL, WADHURST.

DATES OF SALES FOR 1924,

COMMENCING AT 11-30 A.M. (except when otherwise stated)

MONDAY

JANUARY 14th	JUNE 2nd	OCTOBER 20th
JANUARY 28th	JUNE 16th	At One p.m. owing to Rotherfield Fair
FEBRUARY 11th	JUNE 30th	NOVEMBER 3rd
FEBRUARY 25th	JULY 14th	NOVEMBER 17th
MARCH 10th Spring Sheep Sale.	JULY 28th	DECEMBER 1st
MARCH 24th	AUGUST 11th	WED. & THURS. DEC.
APRIL 7th	AUGUST 25th	
APRIL 21st	SEPTEMBER 8th Autumn Sheep Sale	Xmas Show & Sale
MAY 5th	SEPT. 22nd	DECEMBER 15th
MAY 19th	OCTOBER 6th	DECEMBER 29th

Special Sales.

STORE STOCK (Spring)	WEDNESDAY, 9th APRIL
Ditto (Autumn)	WEDNESDAY, 22nd OCTOBER
MAYFIELD FAIR ...	FRIDAY, 30th MAY
Ditto ...	THURSDAY, 13th NOVEMBER
ROTHERFIELD FAIR	WEDNESDAY, 18th JUNE
Ditto ...	MONDAY, 20th OCTOBER

Auction Commissions:—Fat and Store Stock and Cows 1½ per cent. with minimum of 2s.6d. per head. Calves under 45s. 1s. each; 45s. and over, 2s.6d. each. Fat and Store Sheep 1½ per cent. with minimum of 6d. on Sheep and Lambs, and 1s. on Rams. Fat and Store Pigs 2½ per cent. with minimum of 6d. under 20s. Horses 5 per cent. minimum charge 5s; booking fee 2s.6d. returnable if sold. Dead Stock 5 per cent. minimum charge 1s.

ALL BRANCHES OF INSURANCE EFFECTED.   Est. 1873

AUCTION AND ESTATE OFFICES :

Wadhurst (Phone 6) and Heathfield (Phone II)

121. Watsons held sales of stock in the Wadhurst Market Hall and Stock Yard until 1982 - note the phone number in 1924: Wadhurst 6 - now we look for broadband connectivity

122. But not all buying and selling needs to be done in the auction room. Boot sales are a popular affair - this one at Bugsey's Farm in 1990 clearly attracted a good crowd. In a way the boot sale is closer to the earlier mediaeval markets than is our more conventional approach to shopping in stores and supermarkets

123. The St John Ambulance tombola stall at Bugsey's Farm - Peggy Pullen in charge

124. The High Street in 1907

Today we have - on the left above - The Clock House [now King & Co] - Barnett's Bookshop [Gordon House Fashion and earlier - Widow White's School] - T&P [Insurance Brokers] - Newingtons - Ashton Burkinshaw [the old White Hart] - Opticians/Chiropodist/Physiotherapist - Wealden Wholefoods [with pentice over pavement] - Jean Marie - Carillon Cottage - Post Office

On the right - part of Wood-B-Pine and then the buildings have all gone: destroyed by the Meteor crash in 1956 but The Queen's Head shows below on the left

125. And in 1911

126. High Street looking west 1984
Peter Nash - Paint & Decorating
Supplies is now Wealden Wholefoods
and there are far too many cars

127. Again in 1984 - Mrs Graham
in charge. Newingtons continues
in business today

128. Joyce Sharp's Shoe Shop - Closing Down sale 1984
But the shop continues as Jean Marie -selling knitting wool, patterns and
thousands of other items needed by the home dress maker or knitter

129. H C Ford - Butchers of Durgates
Later the shop became The Dairy Shop and now it is
Hambly's Herbal Dispensary and Clinic

130. John Snary - Sparrows Green
Poultry ready for Christmas 1987
[Now John Cook - "Family Butcher and
Local Grazier - Supplier of Fezants Deer &
Partridges direct to the Public - Hotels -
Restaurants & Pubs"]

131. And his Christmas meat
supplies - hanging to mature

132. Ring's Outfitters in 1984
Now Wadhurst Flowers - and Wadhurst lacks a men's outfitters :
some of his shop fittings are in Wealden Whole Foods

133. Animal Feeds
Now The Pet Shop - local stores
seem to change hands and not
always change their business -
see the auctioneers next door :
now Bailys estate agents

134. A Parks Boot & Shoe Repairer, Leather &
Grindery in the High Street
Long gone - but later a restaurant : first The Post
Horn [which burnt out] and now Sonar Gaon

135. E W Howell Dispensing Chemist 1935
Decorated for the Silver Jubilee of George V
selling veterinary & canine medicines as well as
ministering to a human population
Continues as a pharmacy, owned until recently by
the Martel family and now by Paydens of Maidstone

136. R J Luck - High Street 1933
with his wife and daughter - confectioner and tobacconist

137. Wadhurst Ironmongers 1987
Somehow any item you need can be found
somewhere in the shop!

138. The Clock House - 1900 with Harry & Horace Newington

The death of Harry Newington was reported locally: "Wadhurst has lost one of the oldest and most respected residents by the death, which occurred suddenly at his home at Clock House, High Street, on Wednesday last week, of Mr Harry Newington at the age of 88
Affectionately known to all as Clocky Newington, he came from a very old family of clocksmiths, his father carrying on business in the village with his grandfather. His grandfather at one time lived at White House Wadhurst where he had a workshop
Mr Newington came to live at Clock House at the age of nine and when old enough to leave school followed in the family tradition combining the work of a clocksmith with his business of a tobacconist and silversmith
For 60 years he looked after the Parish church clock climbing the belfry stairs three times a week to do this. When he had to give up owing to advancing years in 1955, he was presented with a reading lamp by the Parochial Church Council in recognition of his services. His father commenced to carry out this job when the clock was first installed in 1873, Mr Newington taking over in 1895. He regularly visited a number of the large houses in the district, notably Whiligh, Cousley Wood House and South Park to attend to the clocks
A bellringer for 50 years, he was also a keen musician and was 1st violin in the old Wadhurst orchestra. In his younger days he was a keen sportsman and some of the older inhabitants remember him as a more than useful bowler. Only the day before he died Dr E A C Fazan and his brother called on him and chatted about the days on the cricket field, in those far off days when they used to prepare their own wicket at Hill House
The funeral takes place at Wadhurst on Wednesday April 13th conducted by the Rev D G Newman"

139. Lancasters Florists in
Sparrows Green in 1988
Later moved to the High Street
where Denis & Fiona sadly had to
stop selling flowers

140. Shops at Gloucester Place
Now converted back to domestic
use - fortunately the road block
has been removed

141. Wadhurst Post Office
This became Gobles and is now
Jackie Martel

142. Post Office Staff 1904
back [l to r] Albert Palmer - Shaky Smith - Reg Hayward - George Down - Teddy Rumens
front [centre] Mr & Mrs Casterton : he commissioned some of the old Wadhurst postcards
and note the rocking horse

143. Cousley Wood Post Office
The Old Vine converted the loo into a post office for the
local community - Feb 1988

144. The Mill Feed Company Ltd Sep 1987
Cheesman & Newington became The Mill Feed
Company - the business changed again and again.
Now the site has been cleared for new housing and
conversion of the oast and mill
l to r: Richard Bickersteth - Iris Dipple - Mark Dickens

145. International Stores 1910
A loaded window - now the Post Office

146. The Post Office
Later Gobles and now Jackie Martel : the post boys on
bicycles have not changed much - Hilary still charges
round on her machine delivering letters and keeping fit

In under a hundred years, like so many other buildings in Wadhurst, there have been many major changes in appearance and use in this building, which many commuters probably hardly notice as they drive to or from the station in a rush to catch a train or get home after a hard day in the office

147. W H Newington Stores in 1905

148. In 1909 with its road front properly walled

149. By 1920 known as Bayham Prospect
The store has been extended to the road
and we've moved from bicycles through horse and
cart to motorcycle and sidecar

150. By 1928 the store is beginning to look
run down - and the proprietor looks older!

151. Cleaned up and the upper glazing has
been replaced - now The Station Stores

152. And now the car has had to be provided for
- with parking spaces off the road

153. Today - a family home - called 'Nutshell'

HOUSES GREAT AND SMALL

154. Pennybridge Farm House - Best Beech

Wadhurst is blessed with many fine houses - some dating back to mediaeval times - and with plenty of smaller houses of style and character. But the smallest - agricultural workers' cottages and workmen's terraced houses - are increasingly being bought by commuters to Tunbridge Wells or London with a consequential rise in prices, which is having a damaging impact on the fabric of local society
Traditional construction - timber framing with brick or plaster infill, tile hung or weatherboarded - gives an air of tranquility to the scenery and many of the greater houses are set well back from roads, so do not intrude on the landscape. But the big estates are steadily being broken up - often for re-development of the associated out-buildings : at Castle Park a large-scale build has replaced Pritchards Garage; at Buckhurst Place only the water tower remains - instead seven 'Executive Homes' will occupy the site where Baden-Powell developed some early ideas for scouting

155. Wallands from the air - Stan Cosham's balloon flight July 1990

156. The Old Vicarage - High Street Wadhurst
The house is now a family home with a high
tech business being run in an out-building.
The new vicarage is set behind the Old
Vicarage but still close to the church : much
of the glebe is now the extension to
the churchyard

157. Wadhurst Park - now replaced by a fine modern home

158. Whiligh in 1984 - Mr Hardcastle at the front door and the footmans'
passage at the left - an echo of earlier times!

159. Wadhurst Castle 1925

The Cosham Collection has many examples of auction catalogues for properties in Wadhurst, which shed an interesting light on times past. In September 1920 portions of the Wadhurst Castle Estate were offered for sale - Durgates Lodge and 16 further lots in Durgates, including the land to the east of Jonas Lane, 'The Freehold Ground Rent of £26 Per Annum, secured upon the Important Coachbuilder's and Wheelwright's Premises, Two Capital Dwelling Houses and Yards....let on a 95 years lease from Michaelmas 1905 to Mr J. Bassett' [now a housing development - see 167] and 'a Well-Built Butcher's Shop and Dwelling House with Garden and detached Slaughter House' [now Hambly's Herbal Dispensary]
In July 1925 John D. Wood offered for sale at the Swan Hotel Tunbridge Wells 'The extremely Attractive Wadhurst Castle Estate of some 650 acres including, as a lot of about 65 acres, "Wadhurst Castle" - with 21 bed and dressing rooms, 4 bathrooms...' and electric light
In May 1931 outlying portions of the estate were offered for sale by Bracketts at The Swan, including Windmill Farm, 'Lot 6: the plot of Freehold Building Land of 3 rods 2 perches' sold to Mr Godden the undertaker for £150 - and now the Goddensfield development, and 'Lot 9: The Freehold Ground Rent of £12 per annum secured on Durgates Dairy (formerly Kelsey's Dairy)....held by Mrs Osborne on lease for 99 years from 1901' - the butcher having ceased trading at what is now Hambly's. Lot 13 - 'Freehold Meadow having a frontage to Washwell Lane and an area of 11a. 1r. 38p. let to Mrs Boorman' attracted no bid - but the map shows it had a sheepfold and a sheepwash

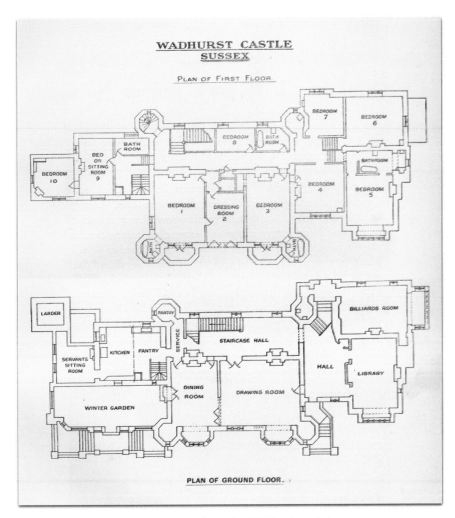

WADHURST CASTLE
SUSSEX

PLAN OF FIRST FLOOR

PLAN OF GROUND FLOOR.

160. Floor plan from the 1936 sale catalogue

In November 1936 Wadhurst Castle and 102 acres were offered for sale by Knight, Frank & Rutley in Hanover Square - 'The Stately Residence, which is of stone in the style of a mediaeval castle with battlemented walls and turrets, has a pleasant and dignified elevation. The interior accommodation has recently been remodelled, with the result that the principal rooms now all face South'

In April 1939 Hampton & Sons were offering 'Wadhurst Castle - a Home of Dignity beautifully positioned in its Parklands extending to over 100 Acres' at auction in London...some three years after the Vendor 'commenced remodelling a greater part of the interior, and being an Architect well versed in domestic architecture, saw to it that everything was done conducive to comfort and convenience.' Watson's copy of the brochure marked a price of £asyyy! What was that in today's money?

161. From the 1925 sale particulars
A small dining table but plenty of
trophies on the walls - and note the
oak panelling and ceiling

THE DINING ROOM—Lot 1.

162. The Drawing Room in 1926
Again note the ceiling and the
heavy sofa

THE DRAWING ROOM—Lot 1.

163. By 1936 the old dining room has become the library and a new dining room constructed in the old drawing room - with use of a 'TURRET ROOM which would be suitable for cards or cocktail bar'

164. The 1936 drawing room - which is described as having a 'TURRET ROOM ....providing useful annexe or accommodation for wireless set or writing room' has been constructed in the old dining room and much lighter furniture is in vogue

The Domestic Offices

are below the Reception Rooms, but are almost on the ground level on the south side, and include :—White-tiled Kitchen with double range, Store Room, Housekeeper's Room, Servants' Hall, Butler's Pantry and Bed Room, Two Bed Rooms for Footmen, Boot and Store Room, Wine and Store Cellars, Separate Hall with two boilers for radiators and domestic hot water respectively.

CENTRAL HEATING, generated by up-to-date Robin Hood boiler is installed.

ELECTRIC LIGHT is generated from an 8 h.p. oil engine with dynamo and 27 cells. The Company's Electric Light Mains are now being laid along the road adjoining the Lodge.

COMPANY'S WATER AND GAS are connected.

THE DRAINAGE is on modern principles, connected to the main sewer of the Ticehurst Rural District Council.

LUGGAGE LIFT.   TELEPHONE.

---

165. Domestic offices at Wadhurst Castle in 1925

166. The 1936 principal dressing room with folding windows 'so arranged that they may be shut back to leave this end of the room almost entirely open to the air, so forming a delightful summer sleeping place'

THE PRINCIPAL DRESSING ROOM
(Showing View through the Folding Windows)

167. Bassett's Forge today

168. 1 - 3 Washwell Lane in 1956 No 3 was the home of Stan & Peggy Cosham - the houses were pulled down to allow the widening of Washwell Lane and the building of the Courthope Avenue houses - you can just see the remains of The Queen's Head after the Meteor crash [243]. The site is now the car park behind One Stop

WADHURST, SUSSEX

In one of the most beautiful positions in the Southern Counties, 570 feet up with southern aspect and magnificent views.

Two miles from Wadhurst Station, six miles from Tunbridge Wells and 40 miles from London.

BEECHLANDS

WADHURST

Family Residence chiefly of modern construction, containing

Ten Bed Rooms, Three Bath Rooms, Hall, Three Sitting Rooms, Excellent Offices, Garages and Stables.

Beautiful Gardens built in Terraces, with ornamental water.

Rock and Bog Gardens.   Kitchen Garden.

The Whole forming one of the most beautiful small Estates in the Country.

About 16½ Acres in all.

Also

SKINNER'S FARM

adjoining, with charming old Sussex Farmhouse, old Oast House and modern Cow-sheds, Barn, Cottage and other buildings.

About 53 Acres of Useful Grazing Land

Also

PIMLICO COTTAGE

a small detached old-fashioned house in a wonderful position, and the accommodation meadow adjoining.

The Whole comprising an Area of about

89 Acres

Main Water and Electric Light.

EARLY POSSESSION OF THE WHOLE.

Messrs. WHATLEY, HILL & COMPANY

are instructed to offer the above (unless sold privately) for Sale by Public Auction in One or Four Lots, at the SWAN HOTEL, PANTILES, TUNBRIDGE WELLS, on FRIDAY, 24th NOVEMBER, 1933, at 4 p.m. punctually.

169. Beechlands - to be sold by auction in November 1933 - with Skinner's Farm, Pimlico Cottage and nearly 11 acres of building land. 'Built by the late Mr. Edward Rayner....an old seventeenth-century building stood on the site...great pains in the layout of the Garden, and all the work was done, it is believed, under the supervision of Mr. Strutt, the well-known artist'

The house became a convent and has recently been converted into a housing complex

170. Beechlands from the south in 1933
With 10 bedrooms, 3 bathrooms, rock &
bog garden in 16½ acres

171. Pimlico Cottage 1933
'A picturesque old-fashioned
cottage'

172. Skinner's Farm 1933
'Admirably suited for a High Class Dairy
Farm and Poultry Farm....The charming
old Sussex Farmhouse....has been
divided into TWO COTTAGES'

173. The Brewery Cottage
Local brewers and inns or public houses were a key feature of rural life but, as transport links developed, amalgamation and consequent closures, and other changes, became the rule. Holmsdale Brewery became a housing development

174. The Greyhound Inn 1904
Continued in business - but the stables [left] are now available for B&B letting to tourists - and the mode of transport has changed somewhat!

175. The Balaclava Inn c 1900
This has only changed its name

176. The Rock Robin 2003
But this looks forlorn as its
future is in doubt

177. Monk's Park
In June 1917 'This valuable freehold residential estate, comprising a commodious COUNTRY MANSION, with excellent buildings and beautiful Grounds, and GATE HOUSE FARM with picturesque Farm House and Model Farmery' was offered in two lots at auction in Tokenhouse Yard, in the City of London by Brackett & Sons

THE GARDENER'S HOUSE,

KNOWN AS

"OLD MONK'S,"

178. The main lot included 'Old Monk's', two entrance lodges, the Bailiff's House and Buckland Hill Cottage and 146 acres 'principally good productive MEADOW AND PASTURE with a suitable quantity of Arable and is divided and broken up by woods (containing oak and other forest trees of mature growth) affording excellent coverts for game'. Land Tax amounted to £8/18/0½, the Impropriate Tithe Rent Charge was £9/4/6 and £6/8/6 was due as Vicarial Tithe Rent. Apportioned quit rent of 2/- was payable in respect of land formerly part of Wick Farm

GATE HOUSE FARM

adjoins the Park. **Its very picturesque half-timbered Farm House** (containing an enormous amount of old oak) includes Attics, Three Bedrooms, Two Sitting Rooms, large Kitchen with ingle nook, Scullery, Dairy and Cellar. Wood Lodge, and Garden.

The First-rate MODEL FARMERY

comprises Stabling for Five Horses, Chaff Room, Cow Sheds for Six Cows, open Cow Lodge for Eight Cows, with feeding passage, Cow Box, Calf Pens, Hay Store, Meal Room, Root House, Barn, Cart Lodge and Granary, Piggeries and Fowl House; all built round a **Large Central Yard.** There is also a Waggon Lodge, and Oast House now used for Storage purposes.

179.　The second lot consisted of 'The Attractive small freehold property NUTLANDS, containing upwards of 6½ acres. The house....contains 4 Bedrooms, Living Room with chimney corner, Sitting Room, Kitchen fitted with small range, copper, etc. Store Room and Dairy. Convenient outbuildings and Pig Pound and timber built Cow Shed with Iron Roof.' The property was let to Mr. George Smith on a yearly tenancy expiring on 29th September 1918. Land Tax of 10/- and an Impropriate Tithe Rent Charge of 13/- were due

180. Site clearance for the car park behind Wadhurst Ironmongers - 1985

181. 1-3 Mews Cottages, Greyhound Lane replaced the old barn above - 1989

182. The Mount School 1987
The old Rosminian Monastery is now a Camphill Community of some 60 people, including co-workers, their children and some 35 students. The main building stands within a 20 acre estate which includes a two acre walled biodynamic (organic) garden and orchards. There are three family-sized houses, one of which was built especially for training in more independent living within the community. The former chapel has been sensitively converted to provide a beautiful community hall - St. Michael's Hall - as well as a library and office facilities.

183. The Drill Hall Lower High Street
Dismantled in 1988 and replaced by the Kingsley Court development

184. Great Shoesmiths Farm
Offered at auction on 20 June 1979
at The Spa Hotel 'Extending in all to
about 216.37 Acres a most
attractive Residential and Farming
Property in a Secluded Valley'

185. The Dining Room
The house originally belonged to the
Barham family of ironmasters; the back
wing appears once to have been an
open hall house c 1500. John Barham
bought it in 1611; his son and
grandson both improved the house
which, in 1760, was sold to Charles
Pratt, later Marquis of Camden

THE PROPER STUDY OF MANKIND - IS MAN

186. James - Jack - Bassett at work in The Forge in Durgates - aged 80

William Courthope commented: 'Tis in vain that we attempt to discover any recognition of the existence of Wadhurst as a parish, either before the Norman Conquest or for a long time after that event : like many of the towns and villages, which have flourished & do flourish in the Weald of Kent & Sussex, it finds no place in the Domesday Record, as the district was within the confines of Andredswald and of little, or no, value beyond the amusement of hunting'

But over the generations it is the people who have made Wadhurst - and who make it what it is today. Some have been among the great and good but those who have made the greatest contribution have been drawn from the bulk of the population. The selection which follows does not pretend to be representative : the Cosham collection of people could fill several volumes on their own - but they have all played a part in Wadhurst life. One or two have appeared elsewhere in print - but are of sufficient interest to reprint here. With few exceptions, we have not included people who are alive today - for that you must go to the later sections of more recent material - up to the Charter Weekend in June 2003

187. Henry Jeffery Austen 1823 - 1887 On his death the local paper recorded:

SUDDEN DEATH OF MR. H. J. AUSTEN

With feelings of profound regret we have to record the death of Mr. Henry Jeffery Austen, auctioneer, which occurred very suddenly on Friday night last. Mr. Austen was in his usual health on Friday morning, and proceeded to his business as usual, which on this occasion lay at Cryalls Farm, Brenchley. After a day's work, taking the inventory for Mr. T. Robert Smith, who is leaving there, he partook of a hearty dinner with that gentleman, who is a teetotaller, Mr. Austen, in his usual social manner, drinking a bottle of ginger beer with him. The ginger beer seemed to upset him, but on his arrival home to Marling Place the ill-effects seemed to pass off, and he then laid on the sofa. He was, however, taken a great deal worse, and before medical assistance could be obtained, we are extremely sorry to say he died. It must have been a dreadful blow to his relatives, but as the news flashed around, every one was sadly surprised, and the sorrow felt is general among every class, rich and poor. Mr. Austen was 63 years of age, and ever since he became of an eligible age for an auctioneer and valuer's licence has most successfully, to the satisfaction of all parties, carried on the business with thorough uprightness and strict integrity of character. His even and genial temperament made him beloved of all classes with whom he came in contact, and he will be sadly missed for miles around. On Sunday, at the parish church, the Rev. C. C. Allen in his sermon spoke of his kindly manner, life of usefulness to his fellow parishioners, and the sympathy of everyone with the family in their bereavement.-The funeral will take place on Tuesday (this day), at the parish church.

The local papers also record that Henry Austen - presumably a widower by then - married the widow of his son's mother. His son's wedding was celebrated with a cricket match:

WEDDING CELEBRATION.-We witnessed an interesting event the other day here, when the workmen on the farms of Messrs J. and D. Tompsett, of Wenbont Farm, and those of Messrs. H. J. Austen and Sons, of Marling Place, met together to play a friendly game of cricket, and to commemorate the marriage of Mr Frank Austen, with Miss Reed, niece of the Messrs. Tompsett's. Both parties in the cricket match were pretty evenly balanced, and a very pleasant game ensured, all seeming to heartily enter into it and thoroughly enjoy themselves : while some veterans were seen handling the bat, who had been resting on their laurels for the past 20 years. The scores were : Mr. D. Tompsett's eleven, 34 and 86, and Mr F. Austen's eleven, 44 and 70. Mr John Tompsett played a not out innings of 53, while on the other side Mr Frank Austen made 43 not out. The match being concluded in favour of Mr. Tompsett's team, the party (numbering 16) adjourned to the Queen's Head Inn, where Host Tulley had provided an excellent and substantial supper, to which full justice was done. The party broke up about 10 o'clock, having spent a most enjoyable holiday which will doubtless be looked back upon by all with a great amount of pleasure. We afterwards had the pleasure of inspecting a valuable present made by the members of the Wadhurst Cricket club to their secretary, Mr Frank Austen, consisting of a very noble and handsome marble dining room clock, striking the hours and half hours in a tone resembling Big Ben, with a plate on the base bearing this inscription : "Presented to Mr Frank Austen, hon. Secretary of the Wadhurst Cricket Club, by the members as a token of their respect and esteem, on the occasion of his marriage, 13th May, 1885." There was also an illuminated address with the list of subscribers, and the owner appeared to be most justly proud of it.

188. Playing on the edge of
The Marlpit
A future generation of Wadhurst
citizens caught by Nugent's
photographer for a postcard -
even for children headgear
seems compulsory
Newington's Grocers - now
Costcutter and - on the right -
the old Fire Station

SPARROW GREEN, WADHURST.

189. The Wadhurst postmaster
and family c. 1890
back: Mary Annie - John Thomas -
Maud - Dora Jane
front: John Thomas Casterton - Ella
Elizabeth - Naomi

190. Millie Reed followed her father in the cobbler's business in the Lower High Street - before WW II

191. The Courthope family at Whiligh 'before 1890'

192. George John Courthope [1848 - 1910] with his
grand-daughter Hilda Beryl [1900 - 1974]
Taken by Joan Courthope c 1905

193. Thomas Barnes [1861 - 1900] with his wife
Alice 1865 - 1947] and their children
Thomas was butler to George Courthope and died
at Whiligh on 25 April
Not all butlers lived in - in the 1840s Courthope
records that William Mann butler at Whiligh lived in
1 Church Street Wadhurst

H. Martin,
Durgates Hill,
Wadhurst.

194. Wadhurst residents we assume - if only
from the photographer's address

195. Jack & Charlie Bassett
Outside The Forge Durgates

196. Rodney Bassett
A third generation - outside The Forge Durgates

197. Celia Hammond
Outside her charity shop CHAT
Once a model always a model

198. George Cosham 7 Jan 1894 - 15 July 1963
May not be a Wadhurst man - but as Stan's father he
should be remembered here

199. Weight Watchers 1989
Still fighting a losing battle Stan
Cosham remains a familiar figure on
the Wadhurst scene

200. Graham Brewster at work
Alex Ross called for 'just a short cut - no styling' : he was
Graham's first customer
For Graham's skill with the clippers - see 291

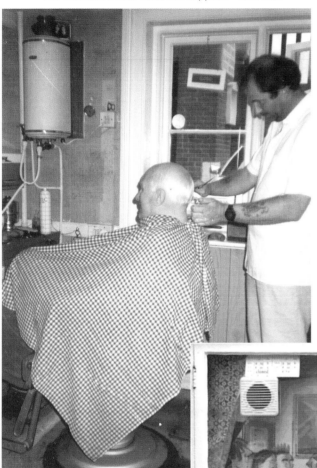

201. Off duty

202. Jack Major
Retired farm worker aged
90 - with his dog Sabar in
Washwell Lane - 1995

203. Sir Henry Cooper and Rosemary Martel at the opening
of the Sparrows Green Sports Centre 9 June 2001

In her role as Chairman of the Wadhurst Parish Council, as a pharmacist
in the High Street and in so many other ways, Rosemary Martel made
an enormous contribution to Wadhurst life - she will be remembered
with affection by so many over the years ahead. Enduring memorials to
her include the Wadhurst/Aubers twinning link and a bench in her
honour in the Jardin d'Aubers, close to the War Memorial

WE TAKE TO THE STREETS

204. The High Street - 1906

Wadhurst does not take to the streets that often - and when it does, the reason is to celebrate and not to protest. We have no history of riotous assembly Today - with the need to obtain permission to close the High Street to traffic - the event has to be particularly significant, like the 750th anniversary in 2003 of the granting of the Market Charter with which this book closes.

In earlier times, processions or street parades were clearly popular; participants and bystanders all having fun and marking each occasion with its own flavour

205. Hospital Sunday procession
- 9 August 1908

The Metropolitan Hospital-Sunday Fund was established in 1873 by the Lord Mayor of
London and religious and hospital leaders
Appalled by the effect of inadequate housing and poor sanitation on impoverished Londoners,
they decided that on one day each year, in places of worship throughout Greater London, a collection
should be made to help improve the health of Londoners
The movement attracted enthusiastic support and spread out from London to Wadhurst and elsewhere

206. And again next year
on Sunday 8 August 1909

207. Empire Day 1909
All in Sunday best - notice the
clock on the side of Newington's

208. Another parade in 1928
Perhaps another Hospital Sunday - notice the new clock

209. Coronation Day 1911
Wadhurst marks the coronation of King George V and Queen Mary with a parade

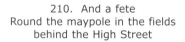

210. And a fete
Round the maypole in the fields
behind the High Street

211. Celebrating in Durgates 1932
But what? Donkeys belonged to
Miss MacDell, and one ridden by
Tom Keeley

212. Silver Jubilee of the accession
of King George V - 1935
Outside Gardner's Stores - now
Threshers Wine Merchants
The back of this postcard says
"Mrs Boorman from Mrs Morgan"

213. Coronation 1935?
St James' Square, by Blacksmiths Lane. A bit of a mystery but a nice picture

214. Feasting in the Commemoration Hall
Perhaps 1953 to celebrate the Coronation of Queen Elizabeth II and the 700th Anniversary of the Granting of our Market Charter

215. Sparrows Green & Tidebrook W.I. - 1969
Golden Jubilee in St George's Hall

216. Silver Jubilee Queen Elizabeth II - 1977
Celebrations in Courthope Avenue

217. Uplands Fete 16 June 1990
Wadhurst seems to be blessed with good weather for its street parades
and festivals : the crowds come out and local organisations have fun
deciding a theme for their entries in the procession

218. 50 years after VE Day
Celebrating in style George Street
enjoys any excuse for a party

219. Young and old alike settle
in for a serious meal

220. To mark the Millennium :
2000 the Uplands disco

221. The White Hart
celebrated from
13:00 until the
early hours

222. Others prepared for the
evening's dance behind the
Social Club

223. The 2002 Scarecrow Weekend Wadhurst Rotary use the scarecrow theme for serious fundraising - the visiting Aubersois must surely have found it all a bit puzzling!

224. Toulouse Lautrec takes advantage of the local supplier of artist's materials

225. 'La guillotine'
Outside the Old Vicarage

226. 'Faux' scarecrow
How he managed to stay quite so still - despite
the curious crowd - remains a mystery

MENS SANA CORPORE SANO

WADHURST SCHOOL.
EAST SUSSEX.
19 38

Measurements, standards and targets are all the rage in the control of education today - but there is little really new in the world. William Courthope quotes the School Report for Wadhurst in 1844:

	On Books	*Present*	*Read with ease*	*with difficulty*
Boys	96	60	9	20
Girls	91	80	17	25

The report continues: 'The first and second class of boys and the first class of girls write on paper; the second class of girls on slate. The first, second and third class of boys and the first and second class of girls know the catechism'

Discrimination in favour of boys is obvious but truancy or other absenteeism is high - boys more than girls : and the consequent higher achievement levels of the girls in school is still apparent today. The picture above [227.] suggests that boys in 1938 were being prepared for an agricultural future

What follows is a small selection of photos covering local sports and education - those wanting more details on the history of our schools should seek out a copy of Kenneth Ascott's book : *The Education of Wadhurst* published by the Book Guild, 1998

Wadhurst School (3)   Coronation year. 1902

228. Wadhurst School in 1902 - Lower High Street
Marking the Coronation of King Edward VII

170. Beechlands from the south in 1933
With 10 bedrooms, 3 bathrooms, rock &
bog garden in 16½ acres

171. Pimlico Cottage 1933
'A picturesque old-fashioned
cottage'

172. Skinner's Farm 1933
'Admirably suited for a High Class Dairy
Farm and Poultry Farm....The charming
old Sussex Farmhouse....has been
divided into TWO COTTAGES'

173. The Brewery Cottage
Local brewers and inns or public houses were a key feature of rural life but, as transport links developed, amalgamation and consequent closures, and other changes, became the rule. Holmsdale Brewery became a housing development

174. The Greyhound Inn 1904
Continued in business - but the stables [left] are now available for B&B letting to tourists - and the mode of transport has changed somewhat!

229. The Eridge Hunt meets at The Greyhound around 1900

230. And again in 1995
Some might argue that fox hunting is neither education nor sport - and
the Government would ban it all together. But fox hunting has been part
of Wadhurst life - adding colour to the local scene

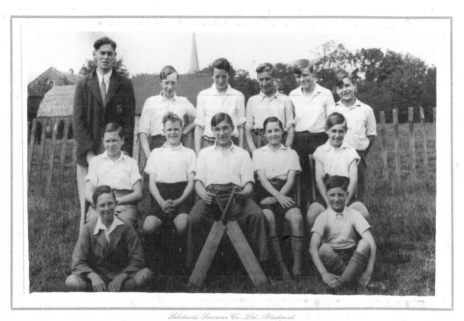

231. 1938 Cricket team
l to r: back row : Mr MacQueen - Arthur Percy - Noel Carney - Vic Blake - Gordon Miller - Fred Galloway
middle : Arhur Freeman - Charlie Tompsett? - Eric Barden - Ron Tompsett - Donald Beeney
front : Freddy Hodges - Ron Thorpe

232. Wadhurst Cricket Club 1984
Preparation is an important part of
the game - Derek Bishop at work

233. But not as important as the aftermath!
John Burgess - Ruth Piper - Fred Crowhurst watch the hog roast

234. Ladies Cricket c 1900
At Whiligh - George Courthope
on right : Joan Courthope took
the photo

235. Wadhurst Cricket Club 1987
l to r : John Burgess - Mark Goldsmith - Alan Borer - Martin Dipple - Gary Bennet - Tim Nelson - John Bishop
Front : Derek Bishop - Julian Plumbley - Richard White - Mick Foster - Richard Griffin

237. Opening the Uplands Swimming Pool
Or are they preparing for the Olympics Synchronised Swimming?

236. Wadhurst Bowls Club
Opening the new pavilion June 1933

238. Wadhurst Primary School children visiting Stan Cosham's museum - 8 May 2003. "It was generally agreed that the museum was just as interesting as the ones in Kensington" said their teacher

239. Wadhurst Hall Football team
Back [l to r] : Billy Anderson - George Collins - Game Keeper - Chauffeur - Groom - Mr Palmer -
Mr Stubbs [electrician] - Gamekeeper - Rev Packard
Seated : Gardener - Len [Game Keeper] - Scotty 'Willie' Anderson - Walter Everest - Groom

Today could any of our big houses field a full team?

240. Wadhurst School Football Team 1933/1934
Mr E Booth [left] - Mr C B Mould [Headmaster - rt]

241. Wadhurst Rangers Under 10s - 1987
Back : Fred Rowley - Clive Gisby
Centre : Wayne Balmer - Daniel Brown -
Ben Mulleneux - Robert Harlow
Front : Mathew Vigor - Keith Rowly - Niki Wilton

242. Uplands School Sports 1972
Robin Eric Stephens - Graham Gordon - Charlie Fuggle - Allister Paydon

WARS STORMS AND OTHER DISASTERS

Wadhurst has generally been fortunate in escaping the worst that can befall a market town: wars have passed us by and riots and civil disturbance have left no trace. The First Great War [1914 - 1918] took its toll : in the battle of Aubers Ridge in May 1915 twenty five Wadhurst men of the Royal Sussex Regiment lost their lives. Wounded soldiers convalesced at Hill House and Belgian refugees were given shelter. World War II [1939 - 1945] also took its toll - the War Memorial has the names of 33 who gave their lives for freedom. Doodlebugs and German bombs also landed in the parish and caused some damage and loss of life

Natural disasters have been few - the worst being the hurricane of 1987 : and we have not escaped man-made disasters too. In 1956 [243. above] an RAF Meteor from North Luffenham crashed on The Queen's Head killing both aircrew and two local residents

The Vicarage,
Wadhurst,

August 22nd, 1915.

Dear

Will you be so kind as to help our "Sand-Bag Fund" by taking some tickets for a GRAND CONCERT in the Market Hall, Wadhurst, on Tuesday evening, August 31st, at 8 p.m. ?

We have been so fortunate as to secure the assistance of several London professional Singers, including Miss MARGARET BALFOUR (of the Queen's Hall Concerts), who are staying in the Parish.

If you cannot come yourself, perhaps you will kindly buy some tickets for our wounded soldiers, Belgian refugees, or others in your neighbourhood ?

We advise you strongly not to miss this Concert.

Please return any of the enclosed tickets you do not want, as soon as possible.

Thanking you in anticipation,

Yours very truly,

(Mrs.) L. S. Stevenson.

Enclosed Tickets @ 2/-. ....

    ,,   ,,   @ 1/-. ....

244. Like her predecessors and successors, the Vicar's wife was active in local affairs - here raising money to help the 'Sandbag Fund' , which was run across the Empire to buy sacking for our troops in the trenches

245. And her son Patric Stevenson was clearly an observant child!

246. Soldiers recuperating outside Hill House 1914 - 1919
staffed by the British Red Cross Society Voluntary Aid Detachment

247. The same scene from the other end - in peacetime
from a postcard issued by E G Couchman - Stationer of Wadhurst
when it was safe to ride a bicycle in the middle of the road!

248. Stan Cosham [l - Royal Army Service Corps] and his brother George [Royal Sussex Regiment] relaxing in Milano in 1945

249. Fire at Tidebrook Place 1963 Not all our disasters hit the national headlines but some clearly catch a photographer's eye

The damaged portion of Tidebrook Place, a girls' boarding school at Wadhurst, Sussex, after a fire which broke out early yesterday.

250. Victorian steam fire engine
Fortunately we no longer have to rely on manpower for beating
fires - this was being taken to the Uplands Fete by
[l to r] Graham Millican - ? - Robert Wilton - Peter Hemsley
Note the moustaches!

251. Wadhurst did not have to rely on steam for too long - on parade at the old Wadhurst Fire Station in Sparrows Green

252. Post Horn restaurant
Seriously damaged by fire in 1982 :
the restaurant re-opened and is now
Sonar Gaon our local good Indian
restaurant

253. Barn fire at Stonebridge
Farm in 1986

254. Blacksmith's Lane Jan 1987 - Stan's wife Peggy

255. Snape Wood 1987
On 16 October 1987, a hurricane hit many parts of England - Wadhurst did not escape. Major damage occurred right across the parish - trees in particular suffered disaster as their leaves magnified the effects of the storm. But boats, buildings and cars suffered too - fortunately the peak of the storm came when people were in bed so we had no loss of life
One positive result - over time - has been the opening up of views across the region. Stan's daughter Marilyn Harlow surveys the damage

256. The Commemoration Hall lost part of its roof

257. And the War Memorial its trees - but the monument escaped

258. Blacksmith's Lane again
Many roads were blocked for a while after the storm but local farmers and the fire brigade worked miracles to get things moving. The real problem was the loss of electricity - power cables were down across the parish and supplies were not restored totally for a fortnight. Crews were brought in from across the country - and the Channel; sadly one man lost his life

259. Cousley Wood Cricket Pavilion - Peter Clifton surveying the damage
The morning after the storm, most people gave up all thought of their normal day's work - but one Cousley Wood lawyer picked up his ditty bag and climbed his way to the station - to express amazement that he could not get a train : hardly surprising with 14 large trees across the line between the station and the first bend south!

260. St John Ambulance really suffered - losing both their key vehicles : their caravan was crushed by a fir tree at Monk's Park

261. Betty Harrison surveys the crushed ambulance

262. In Hook Green before the smaller trees were removed

263. Boats ashore and 264. afloat were wrecked at Bewl on the night of
the hurricane - the dog is clearly puzzled by the S S Francis

THE CLUB AND SOCIAL SCENE

265. 'Dick Whittington' - Wadhurst Youth Club Pantomime 1944

Provided you are willing to join in, there is always something to do in Wadhurst - voluntary clubs and organisations of all kinds offer entertainment and education - from the Aubers Twinning Association to the Youth Club young and old alike need not feel bored.
The selection that follows barely scratches the surface - so our apologies to organisations not covered.
Maybe in a subsequent volume....

266. Wadhurst Bonfire Society
Fancy Dress Competition 1950
Alas no more but Jennifer and Tim
Tunbridge - Brian Gird - Jim Latter -
Charlie Warren - Walter Bone - Ian
Frazer - George Humphrey - Noel
Gibb and Geoff Goldsmith all feature
somewhere here

267. The Cosham Collection - on display at Uplands 1984
l to r : Jayne Harlow - Stan Cosham - Len Young - Charles Bocking [checking on
his rival!] - Mrs Young - Benjamin and Nicola Cluny

Price Sixpence

*Combined Prize Schedule of
Summer and Autumn Shows*

WADHURST GARDENING &
ALLOTMENT ASSOCIATION

SUMMER SHOW

to be held at the

HALL OF COMMEMORATION
WADHURST

SATURDAY 27th JULY 1963

✱ Entries Close Saturday 20th July

COME TO THE ASSOCIATION'S SHOWS AND EXHIBIT
Some surprising entries have been seen during the past
few years. You will also have your produce judged
by competent judges who may consider your
entries better than you yourself realise !

268. Hon. Show Secretary Mr. S. L. Cosham
Entry fees for Non-Members 6d per entry - and a 'Collection of hardy
Vegetables, 5 distinct kinds arranged on a space not exceeding 3ft. x
2ft.3in. may include tomatoes or cucumbers' could win the Challenge
Cup presented by Sir Victor and Lady Schuster **and** 10/-

269. Cup Winners
Miss G Clements - Mrs Pritchard - Mr J Harmer
and Mr Stan Cosham Show Secretary

270. Mothers' Union 1953
Back [l to r] : Mrs Kennard & daughter Audrey - Mrs Casterton - Mrs Newick - Mrs Midmer - Mrs Hope
- Mrs Barnes - Mrs Everdell - Mrs Whyte-Hyde & child
Middle : Elsie Avis - Ivy Sinden - Mrs Noakes - Mrs Smith - Mrs Humphries - Mrs Pilbeam - ? - Mrs Humpries
Front : Mrs Hartnell - ? - ? - Mrs Masters - Mrs Ash-Burner - Mrs Turner - Mrs Goldsmith - Mrs Baldwin
- Mrs Humphreys - Mrs Mercer
On ground : ? - ?

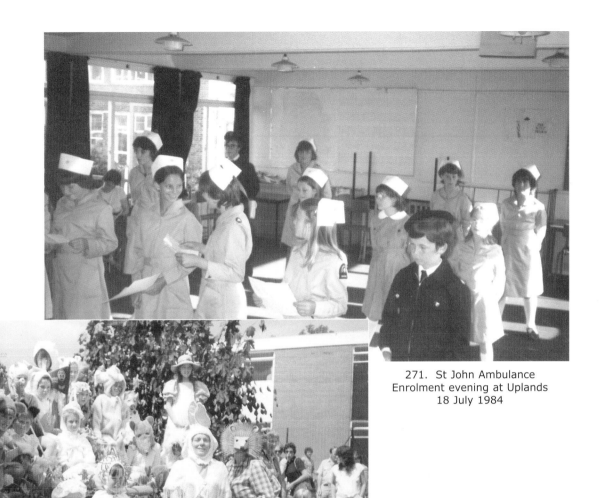

271. St John Ambulance
Enrolment evening at Uplands
18 July 1984

272. Uplands Fete 1985
Wadhurst 2nd year Brownies
on their float - in disguise

273. Wadhurst Sea Cadets 1985
T S Defender - now 'de-commissioned' : the nearest Sea Cadets unit is the T S Brilliant in Albion Road Tunbridge Wells

274. 'Clean Up Day ' 1989
Litter will always be with us - cigarette packets, Kentucky Fried Chicken packaging, drinks cans : but sometimes Wadhurst organises to clear it up

275. Wadhurst Dramatic Club - 'Humpty Dumpty' November 1987

Showing a leg : l to r Heather Woodward - Jenny Pullen - Emma Corcoran - Kate Fenton - Clare Berry - Elaine Stoner

Any selection from the photos of the Club productions would leave some key performers out -
but a full selection would make a book in itself

276. 'Working for Inner City Aid' - Uplands Community College sixth formers - Jan 1988
This group helped restore two old houses in Lambeth
Back [l to r] : Sam Pendlebury - Bob Murray - Mike Watson - Steve Hockley - Jon Swaffer - Mark Goldsmith -
Matthew James
Front : Donna Cirillo - Jo McGregor - Dinah Wood - Jayne Harlow - Kate Jenner

277. CAMEO Club - Christmas lunch 2001
'Come and Meet Each Other' exists to provide a warm and friendly meeting place for senior citizens in Wadhurst - the annual Christmas lunch is just one of the highlights of the year

278. Of course Stan gets everywhere

279. A small army of helpers not only cooks and bottle-washes but also provides transport and other support services for the local community

280. Stan Cosham also runs a 'Hobbies Day' show in the Commemoration Hall - raising money for local good causes In 2001 Michael Harte demonstrated Family History

281. Anthony Cosham his collection of Post Box photos and souvenirs

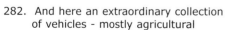

282. And here an extraordinary collection of vehicles - mostly agricultural

CELEBRATING THE WADHURST MARKET CHARTER

Henry by the Grace of God King of England Lord of Ireland Duke of Normandy & Earl of Anjou To the Archbishops Bishops Abbots Priors Earls etc Greeting

Know Ye that We have granted, & do by this our Charter confirm, to the Venerable Father Boniface Archbishop of Canterbury Primate of all England that he and his successors archbishops of Canterbury for ever shall have a Market at Wadhurst in the County of Sussex on the Saturday of each week and that they shall have there a Fair every year to last for three days namely on the Vigil the Day & the Morrow of the Feast of the Apostles Peter & Paul unless such Market & such Fair be to the prejudice of neighbouring Markets & neighbouring Fairs

wherefore we will formally decree for us & our heirs & the aforesaid Boniface & his successors Archbishops of Canterbury for ever shall have a Market at Wadhurst in the County of Sussex on the Saturday of each week & that they shall have there a Fair every year to last for 3 days namely the Vigil, the Day, & the Morrow of the Feast of the Apostles Peter & Paul with all liberties and free usages to such Markets & Fair belonging unless such Market and such Fair be to the prejudice of neighbouring markets & neighbouring Fairs as afores^d.

These being witnessed John Maunsell etc by Our Hand at Westminster the 8th day of May in the 37th year of our Reign

The charter itself was, of course, written in Latin : neither the original - in Lewes Records Office - nor a copy in the Public Records Office at Kew - has survived intact. Written on vellum with silk threads and the King's seal, it measures 6" by 4" and is preserved in a small wooden case. Boniface of Savoy, the uncle of Queen Eleanor of Provence, the wife of King Henry III, was Lord of the Manor of Wadhurst. From 1240 - 1270, he was the Archbishop of Canterbury. He was almost certainly unfairly characterised by William Courthope as "that most rapacious and insolent of prelates". He was clearly close to the King - as he was granted the Market Charter without payment - a rare event in mediaeval times

283. The principal players - Archbishop Boniface
[Brian Bell] and King Henry III [John Phipson]

284. Starting the
celebrations - balloon race
at Uplands : by the end of
term, the furthest travel
was to Margate

285. On 27 June, Sussex Camerata and Polyphony
gave a recital in the Parish Church

286. The 2003 Charter Weekend Programme

Wadhurst celebrated the 750th Anniversary of the granting of its charter with music and song, street processions and market and other mediaeval attractions. The sun shone throughout and 'a good time was had by all'. The following illustrations can give no more than a flavour of the events of the weekend - and a few from 50 years ago show another way of celebrating

287. A craft fair was held in the Commemoration Hall - where local people and our neighbours displayed their wares

288. Stan had his fortune told by Dani Humberstone and Val Brinton outside Meridian Art

289. Paula Bull spun in a mediaeval way - and did not prick her finger

290. Newingtons stayed open for business - Mary Jenner and Valerie Hodgson recalling earlier days

291. Eric Woodward and Michael Harte sold their wares - tonsure courtesy of Graham the Barber

292. Chris Velten carved walking sticks in the midday sun

293. Crowds await the street procession outside the White Hart - refreshing themselves the while

294. With pride of place in the show - Boniface and the King

295. Marking the role of the Parish Church - the vicar, Rev. Jeremy James, carries the cross

Wadhurst Charter Parade

leaves the Sparrows Green Recreation Ground at noon
and will turn down the High Street. Judging will be done at the
Commemoration Hall and on the Uplands Tennis Courts.

Taking part will be :-

Wadhurst Drum and Fife Band

AD33 - 2003	Parish Church
1253	2nd Wadhurst St Peter and St Paul Brownies

Sheep - representing our market.

Mediæval giants and dancers

1703	Wadhurst Methodist Church
19th Century	1st Wadhurst Brownies
1914 - 1918	Twinning Association
1920- 2003	Wadhurst Guides, Rangers and Trefoil Guild
1921 - 2003	Wadhurst W.I.
1927	Wadhurst Probus
1939 - 1940	Wadhurst Primary School
1939 - 1945	Sacred Heart School and Catholic Church
2003	SAP
2003	SSAFA
July 2003	Wadhurst Rotary Club
1253	Sticky Fingers Playgroup
1921 - 2003	British Legion Wadhurst and Tidebrook Branch

Hastings Drum Band

and possibly others.

296. The Full Procession
Floats covered the various aspects of the history of Wadhurst - showing inventiveness
and providing entertainment for all

297. Wadhurst Women's Institute celebrating
82 years of activity - and still going strong

298. SAP
The Social Action Project
provides practical
neighbourly help, on a
short term basis, to
anyone living in
Wadhurst - relying on a
small army of
volunteers

299. 1st Wadhurst Brownies
Enjoying getting dirty - without having to
climb chimneys

300. The Twinning Association celebrated the Battle of Aubers Ridge - that sad event from World War I, which has now enabled a happy liaison with our neighbours across the Channel [La Manche as they will insist on calling it]

301. As ever, music has a major part to play in any festival

302. And ancient crafts still flourish

303. The Hastings Giants

304. Jackie Martel and Jill
Woolnough surely
think they could dress Stan better!

305. A colouring competition gave the youngsters
something to do - and the winner was Georgie Nash
age 11 from Faircrouch Lane

306. And when hungry - try the hog roast

307. And then be entertained

308. Taking care not to become a target in the archery contest - shooting for a purse

309. In 1953 a centre piece of the celebrations was a pageant at Wadhurst Castle telling the history of Wadhurst over the ages

310. They also had a procession through the streets

311. And a re-enactment of the historic fist fight on 10 Dec 1963 between Tom King and John Heenan of the United States - Tom King was knocked out in round eighteen but the fight continued and King won - here B Hemsley and C Pantrey stand in for the original contestants

312. Nicholas Barham visits Wadhurst in 1573 with his wife and friends

313. At the start of the eighteenth century, William Barham the iron master discusses with his foreman designs for his monumental floor slabs

314. Back to the present - the processional entry for St Peter & St Paul

315. Harpist Anna Wynne also entertained in the Parish Church

316. A mediaeval bric-a-brac stall

317. And so it ended - with Stan in a relaxed and happy pose

INDEX TO ILLUSTRATIONS

The index above is to the illustrations making up the separate sections of the book : below is the index to individual places, events and people. To make the index somewhat more friendly, the word Wadhurst has been left out unless it is essential to the sense of the entry

Care has been taken to be as accurate as possible in putting together the captions to the illustrations in this book - but it is almost inevitable that there will some errors : the authors would be pleased to hear of any corrections that should be made to the material in the Cosham Collection

Additional copies of this book are available direct from the authors or from Barnett's Bookshop in Wadhurst High Street : they can also be ordered by phone - 01892 783 292 - or over the internet at www.wadhurst.info\book.htm. Full size - 18 x 12 ½ - and card size - 8 ¾ x 5 ¾ - prints of the frontispiece are also available from the same sources